ESCAPING
SLAVERY

BY PEGGY CARAVANTES

The Child's World®
childsworld.com

Published by The Child's World®
1980 Lookout Drive • Mankato, MN 56003-1705
800-599-READ • www.childsworld.com

Photographs ©: North Wind Picture Archives, cover, 1, 5, 6, 12, 18, 21, 27; Library of
Congress, 9; Red Line Editorial, 11; Chronicle/Alamy, 14; Everett Collection/Newscom,
17; Arthur Bowen Davies/Private Collection/Bridgeman Images, 22; Niday Picture
Library/Alamy, 24; The Print Collector Heritage Images/Newscom, 28

ISBN 9781503825307
LCCN 2017959692

Printed in the United States of America
PA02377

TABLE OF
CONTENTS

FAST FACTS

- There were approximately 3.2 million enslaved people in the United States in 1850.

- There were 18 free states out of 33 before the U.S. Civil War.

- The Underground Railroad was a secret network of people who helped slaves escape from the slave states in the South to the free states in the North.

- Distances between hideouts on the Underground Railroad ranged from 10 to 20 miles (16.1 km to 32.2 km).

- There were more than 3,000 "stations" in the Underground Railroad.

- The Fugitive Slave Act was a federal law that required slaves who escaped to be returned to their owners if they were captured. Approximately 330 black people were forced to return to slavery because of the Act.

- Slavery was finally **abolished** when the 13th Amendment to the Constitution was passed in 1865. However, it was many years before all black people were actually free.

Most slaves in the South were forced to work on ▶ cotton fields.

4

Chapter 1

HENRY BOX BROWN

enry Brown, a Virginia slave, stood on a Richmond, Virginia, street corner with an aching heart as he watched 350 chained slaves walk by. Among them was his pregnant wife, Nancy. With tears streaming down his face, Henry pushed his way toward her, grabbed her hand, and shared words of love. Finally forced to separate, Henry hugged Nancy one last time and looked longingly at his three young children riding in wagons behind the adult slaves. His whole family had been sold to a man in North Carolina. No whipping Henry had ever endured compared with the hurt of this separation.

On that day, Henry vowed to no longer be a slave. Despite the danger involved, he made a plan to escape. Henry decided he would hide in a large wooden box and have himself shipped to a free state. Henry's friend, James Caesar Anthony Smith, who was a free black man, promised to help him. James knew a store owner who could help, a white man named Samuel Alexander Smith.

◄ **Virginia had the largest number of slaves in the United States in the 1860s.**

Samuel believed slavery was wrong. As a **conductor** for the Underground Railroad, Samuel agreed to help Henry escape.

First, Henry needed the right box. Henry choose a large wooden crate and wrote on the top in large letters, "This side up." On another side, Samuel put the address of James Miller McKim, a member of the Anti-Slavery Society. He had agreed to accept the box when it arrived in Philadelphia, Pennsylvania.

THE UNDERGROUND RAILROAD

The Underground Railroad had no trains and no tracks. Rather it was a loosely organized group of people and places designed to help enslaved people escape slavery from the South. "Underground" meant it was a secret. "Railroad" referred to the transportation slaves needed to reach safety. "Conductors" guided escaping slaves in moving from one hideout to the next. Most slaves headed to either the free Northern states or Canada. Underground Railroad sites included such hiding places as basements, cellars, and hidden spaces in walls or furniture. Approximately 100,000 slaves escaped through the Underground Railroad.

▲ The box that Henry hid in was only 3 feet 1 inch (.94 m) wide and 2 feet 6 inches (.76 m) high.

On one of the crate's sides, Henry drilled three holes opposite where his face would be. This provided him air to breathe during the long trip. All Henry planned to take with him was a container of water and some biscuits.

On March 29, 1849, early in the morning, Henry wedged his stout 5-foot, 8-inch (173 cm), 200-pound (90 kg) body into the box. Samuel and James nailed the box shut and tied it with straps.

Stuffed in the box like a sausage, Henry endured the 27-hour trip over 350 miles (563 km) of rail, road, and water. Henry almost died before he reached his **destination**. People handling the box either didn't see or ignored the "This side up" sign. They tipped the box over and left Henry suspended upside down for more than an hour and a half. In the cramped space, he could not move. Henry later wrote that he felt his eyes "swelling as if they would burst from their sockets." Fortunately, two passengers looking for a place to sit down chose Henry's box. They flipped it over, turning Henry right side up.

When the box arrived in Philadelphia, it was placed with the luggage at the depot. There it stayed until approximately 7 p.m., when someone with a wagon came to collect it. The driver took the unopened crate to McKim's address, which was printed on the box. Inside the house, McKim and three other members of the Anti-Slavery Society stared at the box. They wondered if the person inside was dead or alive. Henry kept quiet. He didn't know if he had arrived at the proper address. Then McKim knocked on the crate and asked: "Is all right within?"

Henry replied: "All right."

Using saws and axes, the men removed the lid from the box. A soaking wet Henry tried to stand up. But the long, hot trip had made him weak and **dehydrated**. He fainted to the ground.

When Henry woke up, he rejoiced in the friendly faces around him. They all seemed glad to see him alive. From that day on, he became known as Henry Box Brown, a man who successfully used the Underground Railroad to achieve freedom.

THE UNDERGROUND RAILROAD

Chapter 2

WILLIAM AND ELLEN CRAFT

Married slaves William and Ellen Craft longed to be free. They both lived in Macon, Georgia, but they lived apart because they had different owners. The two constantly feared being sold. Christmas was nearing, and slave owners often gave their favorite slaves time to visit their families. William's and Ellen's owners both gave them three days away from their cabinet-making and **seamstress** work. Instead of taking the time to rest, William and Ellen planned to use those days to escape. They didn't have time to travel only at night as most runaway slaves did. They knew they needed to reach a free state in three days, before their owners noticed they were missing.

Then William had an idea, and the two made a daring plan to escape in full view. Ellen, whose father was white, had very pale skin. They decided to disguise her as a wealthy young white man.

◄ **Some slaves were allowed to have jobs outside of their homes. However, most of their earnings would go to their owners.**

▲ **Ellen, in part of her disguise**

Then William would pose as "his" slave. Ellen dressed in a pair of trousers she had made. Since she could not read nor write, she placed her right arm in a sling to avoid having to sign her name anywhere.

She also needed to hide her smooth facial skin that had no beard. She wrapped a cloth under her chin and over her cheeks. Then she tied it on top of her head. This looked like a **bandage** on her face. William cut her hair straight across the back like a man's haircut. Green glasses and a top hat secretly purchased by William completed her new look.

Ellen and William needed to travel more than 1,000 miles (1,609 km) to safety. The first leg of their journey was 200 miles (322 km) from Macon to Savannah, Georgia. On December 21, 1848, Ellen bought their train tickets. She used money the two had saved from the little they were allowed to keep from their work. The entire trip was filled with danger.

Ellen and William had to ride in separate train cars. Ellen rode in the car reserved for white people. William had to ride in the car for black people. Just as William settled into his seat, he saw his employer from his cabinet-making job looking into the train's windows. William started to panic. He turned his head and slid as low as he could in the seat. Just as the man reached William's car, the engineer clanged a bell, and the train pulled away from the station. William breathed a sigh of relief.

Ellen stared out the window at all the people rushing to the train. When the train started, she turned from the window and gasped. The man sitting next to her was a friend of her owner.

Ellen feared her master had sent the man to bring her back. However, he did not recognize her. Ellen spent the next eight hours pretending to be deaf so that she did not have to talk.

The next leg of the journey was on a steamboat to Charleston, South Carolina. When they arrived in Charleston, Ellen tried to buy train tickets to Philadelphia, Pennsylvania. But the ticket seller insisted she sign a paper proving William was her slave. He would not let them proceed without a **signature**. The captain of the steamboat on which they had just ridden saw what was happening. He said that he knew the "gentleman" and signed his own name for Ellen. Ellen and William then boarded the train, on their way to Pennsylvania, a free state.

On their last major train stop before Philadelphia, a border patrol officer stopped them. He demanded proof William belonged to Ellen. Then a bell rang to signal the train was pulling out of the station. The officer changed his mind. He looked at Ellen's bandages and sling and told a clerk: "Let this gentleman and slave pass. . . . He is not well, it is a pity to stop him."

William and Ellen arrived in Philadelphia the next morning— Christmas Day, 1848. As they left the train, Ellen cried out, "Thank God, William, we are safe."

Black and white people had to ride in different cars on the ▶ train. If a black person had entered the white people's car, he or she would have been in trouble.

Chapter 3

LEWIS WILLIAMS

When Lewis Williams was a young boy, he ran away from his owner, Alexander Marshall, who owned property in Fleming County, Kentucky. For three years Lewis lived as a free person with a friend in Cincinnati, Ohio.

Then Lewis fell in love in his 20s. But he wasn't sure about how the woman felt. He wanted to know if she loved him back. So Lewis contacted a fortune-teller. Lewis revealed to her that he had been a slave and foolishly told her his owner's name and location.

Having the information she wanted, the fortune-teller assured Lewis that his girlfriend loved him. Lewis left happy. But he had no idea the fortune-teller sent a letter to Mr. Marshall. For $200 the fortune-teller offered to tell Marshall where Lewis was.

Marshall rushed to Cincinnati and paid the fortune-teller to give him Lewis's address. A U.S. marshal then arrested Lewis and brought him before a hearing officer. The Fugitive Slave Act of 1850 required proof that a captured black person was a slave.

◀ **Some slaves escaped by crossing the Ohio River from either Kentucky or Virginia to Ohio, a free state.**

A local black preacher, Reverend William Troy, heard what was happening. He often helped escaping slaves. To get assistance for Lewis, he contacted John Joliffe, a white lawyer. Joliffe agreed to take the case free of charge. The two men needed a plan to help Lewis escape. They decided to use the courtroom setting. First, Troy spread the word among the black community to attend the trial. They made sure the courtroom would be packed.

THE FUGITIVE SLAVE ACT OF 1850

The Fugitive Slave Act of 1850 required that all runaway slaves must be returned to their Southern owners. This applied even to those who had reached free states. The law forced private citizens to assist in the capture and return of anyone who had escaped slavery. Captured black people could not have a jury trial, but rather had to appear before a special hearing officer. They were not allowed to speak for themselves at the hearings. The special hearing officers were paid $10 for every black person they returned to slavery. If a slave was freed, the officer was paid only $5. This was to encourage hearing officers to return as many escaped slaves as possible.

▲ **The Fugitive Slave Act was first passed in 1793.**

While the two sides' attorneys carried on a heated argument, Troy noticed in the crowd a young man who looked much like Lewis. That gave Troy an idea. He sought the young man's help. He asked him if he would pose as a **decoy**. He agreed. While the attorneys' argument got louder, the crowd took sides and noise filled the courtroom. Troy motioned to Lewis to slink to the floor. The look-alike was wearing a hat. Troy grabbed the young man's hat and with one hand crammed it on Lewis's head. With the other hand, he shoved the look-alike into the prisoner's chair.

Keeping close to the floor, Lewis crawled to the door, ran outside, and raced toward a forest at the back of the property. As soon as he was gone, the decoy slipped back into the crowd.

When the lawyers' argument finally settled down, the hearing officer realized that Lewis was gone. Someone in the crowd said, "The child left sometime ago; no use to look."

The marshal searched anyway. He offered a $1,000 reward for Lewis's capture. The anti-slavery people banded together to protect Lewis. That night, he moved from the forest to Troy's house. There Lewis was given a new suit of clothes and a haircut to help disguise him. But Troy could have gotten in trouble for protecting a slave. He could have been arrested, fined $1,000, and put in jail for six months. For the safety of both of them, Troy wanted to get Lewis to Canada. He created a disguise for Lewis by borrowing women's clothing from a friend's daughter. She supplied a dress, a skirt, a bonnet, a veil, shoes, and a huge **crinoline** petticoat. Lewis got dressed in the borrowed clothing. When he left the house as a woman, "she" walked through a crowd of people and policemen. No one paid any attention to "her."

For approximately three weeks, Lewis was passed from person to person throughout the Underground Railroad. He covered 300 miles (483 km) across the state and finally reached Cleveland, Ohio. There, Underground Railroad people continued to help him by getting him on a ship bound for Canada. He lived there free for the rest of his life.

Chapter 4

FREDERICK DOUGLASS

Frederick Augustus Washington Bailey was determined to be free. He planned to use his job at a Baltimore shipyard to help him escape. First, he disguised himself as a sailor. He wore a red shirt, a **tarpaulin** hat, and a black scarf tied around his neck. Frederick needed only one more thing—identity papers.

All free black people had to carry papers proving they were free. Since he was a slave, Frederick didn't have such papers. However, all sailors carried a Seaman's Protection Certificate that served the same purpose as free papers. Frederick had a sailor friend who was willing to lend his papers. They included the sailor's name, age, color, height, and build, and any identifying marks, such as scars. Fortunately for Frederick, the borrowed papers did not describe his friend in much detail. However, a close enough look at the papers would have revealed the truth.

◄ **Frederick Douglass first attempted to escape two years earlier, but another slave revealed his plan.**

To prevent the ticket taker from examining the papers closely, Frederick waited to board the train on which he planned to escape. He got a friend to put his luggage on the train. Then Frederick made a flying leap onto the train as it started to pull away from the station. He found his way to the car reserved for black people and sat down.

Frederick waited nervously for the conductor to come to their car to check papers. The risk was great. If he was caught, it would seal his fate forever. He later said: "My whole future depended upon the decision of this conductor."

The conductor only glanced at the sailor's papers and moved on. Frederick's rapidly beating heart slowed as he took deep breaths. But the danger was not over. Several times he saw people on the train he knew.

The first scare came when passengers had to leave the train in Havre de Grace, Maryland, to ride a ferry across the Susquehanna River. Frederick met Nichols, a young man working on the ferry. He was very curious and questioned Frederick so much that Frederick feared detection. Frederick moved to another part of the ferry and crossed the river without further incident.

Back on a train, Frederick noticed two men he knew. One was a ship captain who had employed him in the shipyards.

The captain was on a train headed in the opposite direction from the one Frederick rode. As the trains passed, the captain saw Frederick through the window. But the trains were moving, and there was nothing he could do. The other was a German blacksmith. Frederick later said: "I really believe he knew me, but had not the heart to betray me."

▲ **It was rare for a slave to know how to read and write, but Frederick was taught by his owner's wife when he was young.**

▲ **Frederick later wrote a book about his life called *Narrative of the Life of Frederick Douglass, an American Slave*.**

Despite the heart-stopping near misses, Frederick reached Philadelphia safely. From there he made his way to New York. Frederick had completed his escape in less than 24 hours.

He said: "I felt as one might feel upon escape from a den of hungry lions." His free life began on September 3, 1838, the day he celebrated as his birthday for the rest of his life.

One more change remained for Frederick. By what name would he be known as a free man? With help from a friend, they chose Frederick Douglass, because the friend liked a poem that had a character named Douglas. In later years Frederick Douglass came to be known throughout the world for his speeches and publications, all about the evils of slavery.

THINK ABOUT IT

- Were runaway slaves free once they reached a free state? Give examples from the stories to prove your answer.
- As runaway slaves traveled the Underground Railroad, what are some places that helpful people might have hidden them?
- Slaves risked their lives to escape to freedom. If you were in their shoes, would you take the risk? Why or why not?

GLOSSARY

abolished (uh-BOL-ished): When something is abolished, it is put an end to officially. Slavery was abolished with the 13th Amendment.

bandage (BAN-dij): A bandage is a piece of cloth used to cover an injured part of the body as it heals. Part of Ellen's disguise was a bandage across her face.

conductor (kuhn-DUHK-tur): A conductor was a person in the Underground Railroad who helped slaves escape. Samuel was the conductor who helped Henry escape.

crinoline (KRIN-ul-in): Crinoline is a cloth used to make a skirt stiff. Lewis dressed as a woman in a large crinoline petticoat.

decoy (DEE-koy): A decoy is someone who draws attention away from something. A decoy helped Lewis escape the courthouse.

dehydrated (dee-HYE-dray-ted): When someone is dehydrated, their body is severely lacking in water. After traveling across the country in a box, Henry was weak and dehydrated.

destination (dess-tuh-NAY-shuhn): A destination is the place to which a person is headed. Henry almost died in the box before he reached his destination of Philadelphia.

seamstress (SEEM-stris): A seamstress is a woman who sews, usually for a living. Ellen worked as a seamstress for her owner.

signature (SIG-nuh-chur): A signature is a person's name written by him- or herself. Ellen put her arm in a sling so she wouldn't have to write her signature during her escape.

tarpaulin (tahr-PAW-lin): Tarpaulin is a heavy, waterproof material often used for sailors' hats. Frederick wore a tarpaulin hat to make him look like a sailor.

TO LEARN MORE

Books

McDonough, Yona Zeldis. *What Was the Underground Railroad?* New York, NY: Grosset & Dunlap, 2013.

Robertson, James I. *The Civil War: 1861–1865.* New York, NY: Abbeville Kids, 2016.

Walker, Sally M. *Freedom Song: The Story of Henry "Box" Brown.* New York, NY: HarperCollins, 2012.

Web Sites

Visit our Web site for links about escaping slavery: childsworld.com/links

Note to Parents, Teachers, and Librarians: We routinely verify our Web links to make sure they are safe and active sites. So encourage your readers to check them out!

SELECTED BIBLIOGRAPHY

Craft, William. *Running a Thousand Miles for Freedom.* Athens, GA: University of Georgia Press, 1999. Print.

Douglass, Frederick. *Narrative of the Life of Frederick Douglass, an American Slave.* New York, NY: Barnes and Noble Books, 2005. Print.

Still, William. *The Underground Railroad.* Mineola, NY: Dover Publications, 2007. Print.

INDEX

ABOUT THE AUTHOR

Peggy Caravantes is the award-winning author of more than 25 nonfiction books for children, middle graders, and young adults. She is a retired educator and now spends her days writing, researching, and volunteering for various activities at her church. The mother of three adult children, Caravantes resides in San Antonio, Texas.